Fun Fan Facts:

The Unofficial NBA Edition

Golden State Warriors

Everything Young Warriors Fans Should Know

By: Jake Liam

Dedication

This book is for anyone who has ever watched Stephen Curry warm up before a game and completely forgotten which team they were supposed to be rooting for.

And for every kid in the Bay Area who grew up watching Dub Nation turn Chase Center into the loudest building in California. You inherited something special. Take good care of it.

Dub Nation, this one is yours.

THE NBA BY THE NUMBERS

MOST NBA CHAMPIONSHIPS*

- CELTICS (18) †
- LAKERS (17)
- WARRIORS (7)
- BULLS (6)
- SPURS (5)

As of the 2024-25 Season. † One Trophy = 4 Championships.

NBA HISTORY SNAPSHOT

1946	1954	1979	2023
NBA Founded	Shot Clock Introduced	3-Point Line Added	NBA Cup Introduced

BIG NUMBERS

$156 million
Stephen Curry's est. earnings in the 24-25 season

7'7"
Tallest player in NBA history (Gheorghe Mureșan & Manute Bol)

30 / 4 / 82

30 — Teams Competing in the NBA

4 — Playoff Rounds

82 — Games Per Season

GOLDEN STATE WARRIORS
IN THE NBA

- FOUNDED: 1946 †
- NBA TITLES: 7
- CONFERENCE TITLES: 12 *

5 Consecutive NBA Finals (2015–2019)

*† Founding dates are complicated & may cause arguments at Thanksgiving. Ask someone born before color TV. All Titles reflect pre-relocation franchise history. * As of 2024-25 Season.*

NBA ALL-TIME MVP LEADERS

KAREEM ABDUL-JABBAR (6) ★ MICHAEL JORDAN (5) ★ BILL RUSSELL (5)

EASTERN CONFERENCE

Atlantic – **Celtics**
Atlantic – **Nets**
Atlantic – **Knicks**
Atlantic – **76ers**
Atlantic – **Raptors**
Central – **Bulls**
Central – **Cavaliers**
Central – **Pistons**
Central – **Pacers**
Central – **Bucks**
Southeast – **Hawks**
Southeast – **Hornets**
Southeast – **Heat**
Southeast – **Magic**
Southeast – **Wizards**

WESTERN CONFERENCE

Pacific – **Lakers**
Pacific – **Clippers**
Pacific – **Warriors**
Pacific – **Suns**
Pacific – **Kings**
Northwest – **Nuggets**
Northwest – **Timberwolves**
Northwest – **Thunder**
Northwest – **Trail Blazers**
Northwest – **Jazz**
Southwest – **Mavericks**
Southwest – **Rockets**
Southwest – **Spurs**
Southwest – **Pelicans**
Southwest – **Grizzlies**

Introduction

Welcome, fans! Whether you're new to cheering for the Golden State Warriors or you've been bleeding the team colors your whole life, this book is packed with fun, exciting facts about your favorite team. Get ready to impress your friends and family with everything you know about the Warriors.

Quick Time Out

This book is packed with stats. Like, A LOT of stats. Every fact was checked, double-checked, and triple-checked. But here's the thing about basketball history: not everyone agrees on everything. Ask someone who watched games before color TV and someone who grew up with instant replay and you'll get two completely different answers. My dad, stepdad, uncle, and grandpa all argued about the same fact. Four people. Four answers. All of them think they're right. So if you spot something that doesn't match what you've heard, congratulations. You might be a bigger fan than the people who helped make this book. And honestly? That's pretty cool.

HOW IT WORKS

THE SEASON
82 Games. One Goal.
Each team plays 82 games.
Win enough to make the
Playoffs.
Every game counts!

PLAYOFFS
30 Teams. 16 Make It.
8 per conference make the playoffs.
Win=Advance | Lose=Go Home
Best record
gets home court!

PLAYOFF ROUNDS
Best of 7. Win 4 or Go Home.
4 rounds of pure pressure.
Every series is do-or-die!

OVERTIME?
5 More Minutes.
Keep playing until
someone pulls ahead.
No ties. Ever.

THE FINALS
One Series. One Champion.
Winner lifts the Trophy.
Legend status unlocked.

How the NBA Works

At first glance, basketball feels simple. Ten players. One ball. Two hoops. Go.

Then the NBA adds the layers.

An 82-game regular season. A draft where bad teams pick first. Playoffs that last two full months. Superstars who can change everything with one trade. Dynasties that rise, fall, and rise again.

And somehow, it all works.

The NBA is built on one big idea: every team gets a chance to reset, reload, and rise again. No relegation. No dropping down to a lower league. Just basketball, every night, from October through June.

It is a league designed for drama, stars, and comebacks. And once you understand the flow, it is impossible to stop watching.

The League Setup

The NBA has 30 teams, spread across the United States and Canada. Those teams are split into two conferences:

- Eastern Conference
- Western Conference

Each conference has three divisions, mostly based on geography. Divisions matter for scheduling, but not as much as they used to.

Every team plays 82 regular season games, usually from October through April. Home games. Road games. Back-to-back nights. Long road trips. The season is a marathon before the sprint even starts.

Win games, and you climb the standings. Lose too many, and the pressure builds fast.

How Games Are Played

An NBA game has four quarters, each lasting 12 minutes. That means 48 minutes of game time, plus timeouts, free throws, and the occasional coach argument that adds another 20 minutes nobody planned for.

Scoring is simple:

- A shot inside the three-point line is worth 2 points
- A shot beyond the arc is worth 3 points
- Free throws are worth 1 point

If the score is tied at the end of regulation, the game goes to overtime, which lasts 5 minutes. Still tied? Another overtime. Keep going until someone wins.

There is a shot clock too. Teams have 24 seconds to take a shot. No standing around. No holding the ball forever. Keep it moving.

The Regular Season Race

The regular season is long for a reason. It tests everything.

Depth. Health. Focus. Patience.

Teams play opponents from both conferences, but they face conference rivals more often. By the end of the season, each conference's top teams have earned their playoff spots the hard way.

The goal is simple: make the playoffs. But there is a twist.

The NBA Cup

In 2023, the NBA added something new to the middle of the season. Something with actual stakes. They called it the In-Season Tournament, now known as the NBA Cup.

It works like this: Every team plays a small group stage during November and December, with special court designs that look like nothing else in basketball. The best teams advance to a knockout round held in Las Vegas.

The winners split a prize pool. Players earn bonus money. And for the first time, a team could lift a trophy before the playoffs even started.

Some fans are still warming up to it. Some players love it. But the moment a team starts treating it seriously and a crowd shows up buzzing in December, it feels like something.

Which, honestly, sounds about right.

The Play-In Tournament

Instead of sending the top eight teams from each conference straight to the playoffs, the NBA added something new. The Play-In Tournament.

Here is how it works:

- Teams ranked 1 through 6 in each conference are safe
- Teams ranked 7 through 10 fight for the final two playoff spots

The 7 and 8 seeds have an advantage. Win once and you are in. Lose and you still get one more shot. The 9 and 10 seeds have to win twice in a row just to earn a first-round matchup.

It turns the end of the season into a sprint. Every game suddenly matters more. Fans love it. Coaches age rapidly.

The NBA Playoffs

Once the playoffs begin, everything tightens.

Sixteen teams enter. Eight from each conference. Every round is a best-of-seven games series. That means the first team to win four games moves on:

- First Round
- Conference Semifinals
- Conference Finals
- NBA Finals

Home-court advantage matters. Crowds get louder. Rotations get shorter. Superstars play heavier minutes. One bad quarter can flip a series. One great performance can define a career.

By the time the NBA Finals arrive in June, only two teams are left. One from the East. One from the West. Four wins away from a championship. Four wins away from history.

The NBA Draft: Hope Begins Here

Here is where the NBA gets clever. Every summer, new players enter the league through the NBA Draft. Teams take turns selecting college players, international stars, and teenagers straight out of high school.

The teams that finished with the worst records get the best odds to pick early through the Draft Lottery. It is not guaranteed, but it gives struggling franchises a real shot at changing their future with one pick.

That means one bad season does not doom you forever. It might actually change everything. Some franchises are rebuilt by a single draft night moment.

Hope shows up wearing a new jersey.

No Relegation. All Pressure.

Unlike many global sports leagues, NBA teams never drop down to a lower league. They always stay in the NBA.

That does not mean there is no pressure.

Fans remember losing seasons. Owners make changes. Coaches get replaced. Players get traded. Every year is a test of direction, patience, and belief.

Stars, Systems, and Showtime

The NBA is famous for its stars. But stars do not win alone.

Teams need chemistry. Coaches need systems. Role players need to deliver on the biggest stages. One injury. One hot streak. One trade deadline deal. Any of it can flip a season.

That balance between individual brilliance and team basketball is what makes the league special.

Fast breaks. Buzzer-beaters. Game 7s. And moments that get replayed forever. That is the NBA.

Once you get the flow, it is pure electricity.

Golden State Warriors Facts

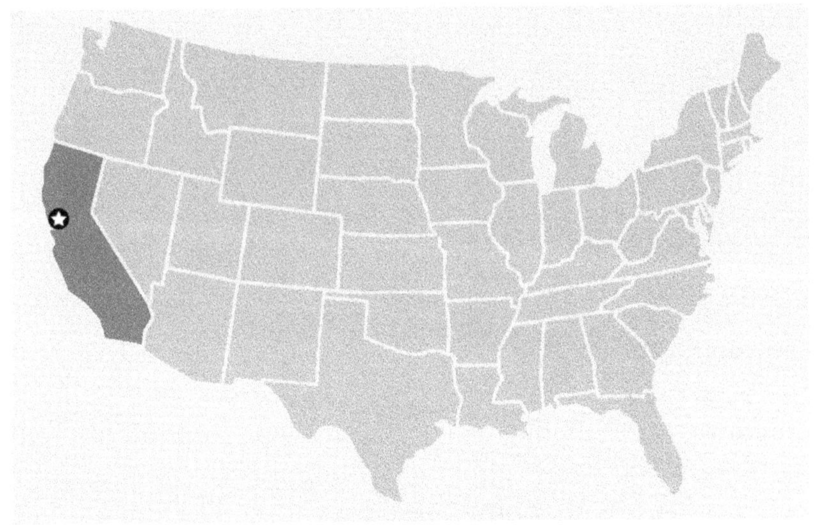

Home City

San Francisco, California

Metro Area Population

About 4.7 Million

Home Arena

Chase Center

Arena Capacity

18,064

Conference / Division

Western Conference / Pacific Division

Famous Local Food

Sourdough Bread, Dungeness Crab, Mission Burritos,
Clam Chowder Bread Bowl

Chapter 1: From Philly to the Bay

1. The Very First Champions: How It All Started (1946)

Before Golden State, before San Francisco, before any of it, there were the Philadelphia Warriors. And before the NBA even had a name people recognized, the Warriors were already winning. The Basketball Association of America launched in 1946, and in its very first season, the Philadelphia Warriors won the whole thing. First year. First ring. No waiting around.

The man who made it happen was a forward named Joe Fulks, and Joe Fulks was absolutely unhinged in the best possible way. He averaged 23.2 points per game in a league where most players were happy to score ten. That might not sound wild until you realize basketball in 1947 looked nothing like it does today. Players did not really jump-shoot. They set their feet, aimed carefully, and hoped for the best. Fulks launched from all over the court like he had somewhere else to be. People called him "Jumpin' Joe" and spent most of his career not knowing what to do about him.

So here is the thing about the Golden State Warriors that most fans do not know: this franchise is older than your grandparents' favorite TV shows. They were not just early to the party. They were the party. Seven championships later, it all traces back to a guy named Jumpin' Joe in 1947. Not a bad way to start a legacy.

2. Wilt the Stilt Arrives and Breaks Everything (1959-1965)

Before Wilt, there was one other player so unstoppable that the NBA panicked and changed its own rules to slow him down. He played for a different team, wore thick glasses, and if you want the full story, you're going to need to get the Lakers book. But here is the short version: the league widened the lane once because of that guy. Then Wilt Chamberlain arrived in 1959, and they had to widen it again.

Wilt averaged 41.5 points and 25.1 rebounds per game across his time with the Warriors. His single-season scoring average of 50.4 points in 1961-62 is an NBA record that has never been touched. For comparison, a player who averages 25 points today is considered one of the best scorers in the league. Wilt averaged double that. It is like showing up to a spelling bee and reciting the entire dictionary. Teams tried double-teaming him, triple-teaming him, and sending the entire roster at him. He still scored. He still rebounded.

The NBA changed its rules multiple times specifically because of Wilt, including widening the lane yet again to push him further from the basket. He adjusted and kept dominating. They also changed the rules around inbounding the ball after a made free throw because Wilt had figured out how to catch the ball before it hit the ground and tap it back in. The league essentially played a game of whack-a-mole with his advantages and lost every round. Two players in NBA history were so good they forced a rewrite of the rulebook. Wilt was one of them. The other one? Go grab the Lakers book.

3. The 100-Point Game: A Record Nobody Has Touched (1962)

On March 2, 1962, in a regular-season game played not in Philadelphia, not in an NBA arena, but in a minor-league hockey rink in Hershey, Pennsylvania, Wilt Chamberlain scored 100 points. One hundred. In one game. Against one team. The New York Knicks had no answers, no solutions, and apparently no way to stop what was happening to them for 48 consecutive minutes.

Imagine this: you are a Knicks defender in 1962. Your job tonight is to guard Wilt Chamberlain. You have tried everything. You have fronted him. You have doubled him. You have fouled him so many times your hands hurt. It is the fourth quarter. He already has 89 points. Your coach has no timeouts left. The crowd is chanting. You look at Wilt. Wilt looks at you. There is nothing left to do.

There was no television broadcast of the game, which means the only proof it happened is a locker room photo of Wilt holding a piece of paper with "100" written on it in marker. That photo is now one of the most famous images in sports history. The record has stood for more than 60 years and counting. The 100-point game is not just a record. It is a message from history that says: you were not there, but you should know this happened.

4. Heading West: Three Cities, One Team (1962-1971)

The Philadelphia Warriors became the San Francisco Warriors in 1962, which was a bigger deal than it sounds. Moving a professional sports team across the entire country in the early 1960s was not a simple logistical exercise. There were no charter flights, no massive support staffs, and very little infrastructure waiting on the other side. A group of Bay Area investors bought the franchise, put it on a plane, and hoped California would care about basketball.

California cared, eventually. But the early San Francisco years were a bumpy ride. The team played at a venue called the Cow Palace, which is exactly what it sounds like. It was a multi-purpose arena in Daly City that had hosted livestock shows and rodeos before the Warriors showed up. The players dressed in a building that smelled exactly like you would expect a building full of cows and horses to smell. Professional basketball players, preparing for NBA games, in a room that previously held livestock. The Warriors made it work. The smell did not make it easy.

In 1971, the team rebranded as the Golden State Warriors to represent the whole state of California rather than just San Francisco. That name stuck. The

Warriors would eventually land in Oakland, build a fan base that became one of the loudest and most loyal in the NBA, and then, decades later, cross the bay to San Francisco again with a brand-new arena. Three cities. One franchise. Seven championships. Did you know that the Warriors are one of only three surviving founding members of the NBA? They were there at the very beginning, and they are still here. That is not luck. That is longevity.

5. The 1975 Sweep Nobody Saw Coming (Rick Barry's Masterpiece)

The 1975 NBA Finals might be the single biggest upset in league history. The Golden State Warriors, seeded fourth in the Western Conference, went up against the Washington Bullets, who had the best record in the Eastern Conference and were heavy favorites to win the championship. The experts picked Washington. The bookmakers picked Washington. Pretty much everyone picked Washington. Nobody told the Warriors.

Golden State swept the Bullets four games to zero. Not a close series. Not a "we scratched and clawed to a game seven" situation. A sweep. The Warriors dismantled Washington with speed, defense, and the brilliance of Rick Barry, who averaged 29.5 points, 4 assists, and 3.5 steals during the series and won Finals MVP going away. Barry was the kind of player who made basketball look like a problem only he understood how to solve.

The coach of that Warriors team was Al Attles, a former Warrior player who had been with the franchise since the early 1960s. He was only 38 years old when he led his team to the title. Attles later became the Warriors' general manager and ambassador, staying connected to the franchise for more than five decades. The 1975 championship is often overlooked because it came sandwiched between the flashier eras of Wilt and Curry. That is a shame. Because what happened in those four games against Washington is proof that the Warriors have always known how to win when nobody was paying attention.

6. Stephen Curry: The Greatest Shooter Who Ever Lived (2009-present)

There is a debate in basketball about who the greatest shooter of all time is. The debate is very short. It starts and ends with Stephen Curry, and everyone else is competing for second place. Curry has made more three-pointers than any player in NBA history. He has broken his own single-season three-point record three times. He has won four championships, two MVPs, one of them unanimous, and an Olympic gold medal. He has also fundamentally changed how basketball is played at every level from the NBA down to rec leagues full of grown adults who definitely should not be launching shots from 35 feet.

Curry grew up as the son of an NBA player, Dell Curry, and was told by almost every college scout that he was too small and too weak to play at the highest level. Davidson College took a chance on him when the bigger programs passed. He led Davidson on a stunning NCAA Tournament run in 2008 that made the entire country take notice. When the Warriors drafted him seventh overall in 2009, some people thought it was a reach.

Those people have had a lot of time to think about being wrong.

What makes Curry different is not just the range, though the range is genuinely absurd. He regularly makes shots from distances that other players would not attempt in practice. What makes him special is the speed of his release. He catches, sets, and shoots in less time than most players need to decide whether to shoot. Defenders know the shot is coming and still cannot stop it. That is not just skill. That is a different category of human.

7. Klay Thompson: The Other Splash Brother (2011-2024)

On any other team in any other era, Klay Thompson would have been the best player on the roster. With Golden State, he was the second-best shooter on his own squad, and even that did not slow him down. Together, Curry and Thompson became the most feared shooting duo in NBA history, nicknamed the Splash Brothers because the only sound that followed their shots was the net going swish.

Thompson's greatest single performance came on January 23, 2015, against the Sacramento Kings. In the third quarter of that game, he scored 37 points. Not 37 for the game. Thirty-seven in one quarter. Fourteen minutes of basketball. He made 13 of 13 shots from the field, nine of nine from three-point range, and did not miss once. The Kings could not foul him into a mistake. They could not switch their defense fast enough. They could not do anything except watch and wait for the quarter to be over. It remains the most points ever scored in a single quarter in NBA history.

Then came the injuries. A torn ACL in 2019. A torn Achilles in 2020. Back-to-back seasons, back-to-back devastating setbacks. Most players do not return from one of those injuries at full strength. Klay came back from both and won a fourth championship in 2022. In the summer of 2024 he signed with the Dallas Mavericks, ending his run in Golden State. He left as one of the most decorated Warriors in franchise history, with four rings, five All-Star appearances, and one quarter that nobody will ever forget.

8. Draymond Green: The Engine Nobody Talks About Enough (2012-present)

If Stephen Curry is the face of the Warriors dynasty and Klay Thompson is the other face, then Draymond Green is the neck, the spine, and probably the whole skeleton underneath. He does not lead the team in scoring. He never has. He makes the entire team work, and without him, none of the championships happen. Full stop.

Green was drafted 35th overall in 2012, which means Golden State got him in the second round. Teams that passed on him in the first round have had a lot of time to think about that decision too. At six feet six and built like a piece of furniture, Green plays every position depending on what the team needs. He guards point guards. He guards centers. He directs traffic on defense like an air traffic controller who is also somehow playing the game. He sees passes before they exist. He communicates with teammates at a speed that most coaches cannot keep up with.

Did you know that Draymond Green led the league in assists in 2016-17 as a power forward? That almost never happens. Big men collect rebounds and score inside. Green was running the offense from the four spot. He has also been one of the most technically skilled defenders of his generation, making four All-Defensive First Teams. None of this shows up cleanly in the box score, which is exactly why casual fans underestimate him and every coach in the league knows exactly how valuable he is. The Warriors without Draymond Green are a very good team. The Warriors with him are a dynasty.

9. Wilt Chamberlain: The Most Unstoppable Warrior (1959-1965)

We talked about the 100-point game in Chapter 1. That was just one night. The rest of Wilt Chamberlain's career with the Warriors was equally unreal, just spread across six seasons instead of one memorable evening in Hershey, Pennsylvania.

Wilt averaged 41.5 points and 25.1 rebounds per game across his time with the franchise. To put the rebounding number in some kind of human context: the NBA rebounding leader today typically averages somewhere around 13 or 14 boards per game, and that player is celebrated as one of the best rebounders in the league. Wilt averaged 25.1. He grabbed nearly twice as many rebounds per game as the best rebounders in modern basketball. He did this while also being the leading scorer. He did it against players who were specifically trying to stop him. The gap between Wilt and everyone else was not a gap. It was a canyon.

Pretend for a minute that you are a forward in the early 1960s. Your assignment is to rebound against Wilt Chamberlain. You have positioned yourself well. You have inside position. You jump at exactly the right moment. You reach as high as your body will allow. Wilt catches the ball six inches above your outstretched hand. He looks down at you the way a lighthouse looks down at a rowboat. He does not say anything. He does not need to.

The Warriors traded Wilt to Philadelphia in 1965 and immediately went from 48 wins to 17. That is what happens when you trade a force of nature.

10. Rick Barry: The Underhand Legend (1965-1967, 1972-1978)

Rick Barry shot his free throws underhand. Granny style. With both hands. He released the ball in a soft, looping arc that looked nothing like anyone else in the NBA. His teammates probably gave him grief about it. Fans in opposing arenas definitely gave him grief about it. None of it mattered, because Rick Barry made 89.3 percent of his free throws for his career, which ranks among the best percentages in NBA history.

Barry arrived as a first-round pick in 1965 and immediately became one of the most complete forwards in the game. He could score from anywhere. He defended like it was personal. He averaged 29.5 points during the 1966-67 season and led the league in scoring. Then things got complicated. A contract dispute sent him to the ABA for four seasons, and Warriors fans had to watch their best player perform for the rival Oakland Oaks while not being allowed to watch their own team win. It was not ideal.

When Barry came back to Golden State in 1972, he picked up right where he left off. And in 1975, he delivered the greatest performance in Warriors championship history, carrying the team through a

Finals sweep and earning MVP honors. He is the only player in professional basketball history to lead the NCAA, ABA, and NBA in scoring. Three different leagues. Three scoring titles. One very unusual free throw. Some people look at the underhand technique and think it looks silly. Rick Barry looks at four rings and lets the trophies do the talking.

Rick Barry rises with smooth control, eyes locked on the rim. Confidence. Precision. Barry led the Golden State Warriors to the 1975 NBA Finals, where they shocked the basketball world by sweeping the powerful Washington

Bullets. Barry was named Finals MVP and became one of the most fearless scorers of his era. *Photo: Rick Barry, Warriors (1). Photograph via Wikimedia Commons. Licensed under CC BY-SA 2.0. Source: Wikimedia Commons.*

11. "We Believe": The Upset That Woke Up the Bay (2007)

In 2007, the Golden State Warriors had not made the playoffs in thirteen years. Thirteen. That is longer than most kids reading this book have been alive. The Warriors were a fun team with exciting players, but fun and exciting does not always mean winning. Then they sneaked into the playoffs as the eighth seed and drew the Dallas Mavericks in the first round. The Mavericks had won 67 games that season. They were the best team in the NBA. The Warriors were supposed to lose politely and go home.

Apparently, being the underdog with nothing to lose was a Golden State specialty. They had done it before in 1975, and nobody had learned the lesson.

Baron Davis, the Warriors' point guard, played those playoffs like a man who had been personally insulted by the concept of losing. He threw down dunks that made highlight reels for years. He hit shots from distances that had no business going in. The Warriors won the series four games to two, pulling off one of the biggest upsets in NBA playoff history. The Mavericks, the best team in basketball, went home. The Warriors, the team nobody picked, kept playing.

The slogan that season was "We Believe." It started with fans and took over the entire Bay Area. Signs in windows. T-shirts everywhere. A city that had waited thirteen years finally had something to cheer about. The 2007 Warriors did not win the championship. They lost in the second round. But that team planted a seed. It showed the Bay what Golden State basketball could feel like when everything clicked. Eight years later, that seed grew into a dynasty.

12. The 73-9 Season: The Best Record in NBA History (2015-16)

The 1995-96 Chicago Bulls went 72-10. For twenty years, that was the gold standard of regular season dominance. Michael Jordan. Scottie Pippen. The best record ever. Untouchable. Then the Golden State Warriors went 73-9 in 2015-16 and took that record away, and if you want the full story on the Bulls side of things, you are going to need to find the Chicago Bulls book.

Seventy-three wins. Nine losses. In an 82-game season. That means the Warriors lost roughly once every nine games. Stephen Curry was the engine of the whole thing, winning his second consecutive MVP award and becoming the first unanimous MVP in NBA history, meaning every single voter picked him first. Not most voters. Every voter. That does not happen.

Curry set the all-time record for three-pointers made in a season that year with 402. He had broken the record the year before with 286. Before Curry, nobody had ever made 300 in a season. He made 402. The gap between him and the previous record holder was larger than the gap between most shooters and him. Here is the twist, though: the Warriors won all those games and then lost the Finals to LeBron James and the Cleveland Cavaliers in seven games after leading three games to one. The best regular season in NBA history ended without a championship. Sometimes the universe has a sense of humor. Not a great one.

13. Kevin Durant Joins the Party (and Wins Two Rings) (2016-2019)

After losing the 2016 Finals while leading three games to one, the Warriors did something unprecedented. They added Kevin Durant. Durant had just finished losing to Golden State in the Western Conference Finals. He was a former MVP, a scoring machine, and one of the five best players on the planet. He signed with Golden State in the summer of 2016 and the basketball world collectively lost its mind.

Travel back to the summer of 2016. You are a casual NBA fan who checks the stats on occasion. You wake up on July 4th and check your phone. Kevin Durant has signed with the Golden State Warriors. The team that just went 73-9. The team with Stephen Curry and Klay Thompson and Draymond Green. You put your phone down. You pick it up again. It still says the same thing. You go back to sleep and hope it is a dream. It is not a dream.

The Warriors won the championship in 2017 and 2018 with Durant on the roster. Both times they were nearly unstoppable. In the 2017 Finals they swept LeBron's Cavaliers. In 2018 they beat them again in four games. Durant won Finals MVP both years. The partnership worked exactly as advertised. Then in Game 5 of the 2019 Finals, Durant ruptured his Achilles tendon and the whole thing unravelled. He left for the Brooklyn Nets that summer. The dynasty continued without him, but Golden State and Kevin Durant had delivered two of the most dominant championship runs the league had seen in decades.

14. Klay Thompson's 37-Point Quarter: One Quarter. One Record. Forever. (2015)

We covered Klay Thompson's career in Chapter 2, but this moment deserves its own spotlight because it is genuinely one of the most ridiculous things that has ever happened in a basketball game. On January 23, 2015, in a game against the Sacramento Kings that the Warriors were already winning, Klay Thompson caught fire in the third quarter and refused to stop.

Thirteen of thirteen from the field. Nine of nine from three-point range. Thirty-seven points in fourteen minutes of basketball. There was a stretch where the Kings tried switching their defense, then doubling him, then switching again, and none of it mattered because Klay was in a zone that exists somewhere beyond the reach of normal defensive strategies. His teammates mostly stood and watched because getting in the way felt dangerous.

The NBA record for points in a quarter before that night was 33. Klay beat it by four points while missing zero shots. Zero. The Kings scored 25 points as a team in that same quarter. One man outscored the entire opposing roster in a quarter and had four points to spare. If basketball has a cheat code, Klay Thompson found it that night in Sacramento and used it for fourteen straight minutes until somebody finally turned off the game.

15. The Dynasty: Four Titles, Five Finals, One Golden Era (2015-2022)

Between 2015 and 2019, the Golden State Warriors went to five consecutive NBA Finals. Five. In a row. No team had done that since the Bill Russell Celtics in the 1960s. They won three of those five. Then in 2022, they came back after three years of injuries and roster changes and won a fourth championship. Four titles in eight years, which puts the Warriors in a conversation with the greatest dynasties in professional sports history.

What made the dynasty special was not just the winning. Plenty of teams win. What made Golden State different was how they won. They played a style of basketball that the entire league scrambled to copy. Ball movement. Perimeter shooting. Small-ball lineups that confused defenses. Players who passed and moved and shot from anywhere on the court. Before the Warriors, teams built their offenses around getting the ball inside to a big man. After the Warriors, everyone started hunting three-pointers and spacing the floor. They did not just win championships. They changed the sport.

The four championship teams from 2015 to 2022 also built something rarer than trophies. They built a genuine team. Curry, Thompson, and Green came up through the organization together. They went through losing seasons together. They won together. They survived injuries and roster changes and the Durant experiment together. In an era when superstars jump from team to team chasing rings, three guys stuck around and built something that will be talked about for as long as basketball is played. That is not nothing. That is actually everything.

16. "Strength in Numbers": The Motto That Meant It

Every team in the NBA has a slogan or a motto or a catchphrase. Most of them mean nothing. They are marketing words invented by someone in an office who has never played basketball. "Strength in Numbers" was different. It was not invented by a marketing department. It grew out of how the Warriors actually played, and it captured something real about what made that team special.

The idea was simple: Golden State did not win because of one superstar. They won because of depth, ball movement, and the fact that on any given night a different player could take over. Stephen Curry was the best player. But Klay Thompson could erupt for 37 points in a quarter. Draymond Green could control a game without scoring 10 points. Andre Iguodala could shut down the best player on the other team. Harrison Barnes could hit a big shot. Shaun Livingston could run the second unit like a professional chess player.

The numbers on the scoreboard reflected the whole roster, not just one name. In the 2015 Finals, Andre

Iguodala won Finals MVP over Stephen Curry, which had never happened before. The best player on the team did not win the award because a different player was even better in the actual series. That is "Strength in Numbers" in one sentence. The motto fit on a T-shirt. It also happened to be literally true, which is the best kind of slogan to have.

17. Run TMC: The Most Fun Team That Never Won a Ring (1989-1991)

Before the Splash Brothers, before the dynasty, before any of it, there was Run TMC. Tim Hardaway. Mitch Richmond. Chris Mullin. Three of the most entertaining players in the NBA crammed onto the same roster in the late 1980s and early 1990s, and the result was one of the most fun teams in Warriors history even though they never won a single championship.

The nickname came from the hip-hop group Run DMC, which tells you everything you need to know about the era. These were not slow, methodical players who ground out wins with defense and discipline. They ran. They shot. They scored in bunches and dared the other team to keep up. Hardaway had a crossover dribble so vicious it looked illegal and probably should have been.

Richmond could score from anywhere. Mullin was pure, silky smooth, the kind of shooter who made the game look effortless.

Chris Mullin played for Golden State for nine seasons and scored more than 16,000 points for the franchise. He was a five-time All-Star and had his jersey retired by the Warriors. Hardaway and Richmond both became Hall of Famers after their careers ended. Three Hall of Famers. One team. Zero rings. Sometimes the timing just does not work out. Run TMC was beloved in the Bay Area not because they won everything but because they played like they were genuinely having the time of their lives every single night. In a franchise full of great teams, they deserve their own chapter in the story.

18. Chase Center: The Billion-Dollar Home They Built Themselves

In 2019, the Golden State Warriors opened Chase Center in San Francisco. It is a beautiful modern arena right on the waterfront, with views of the bay and a design that feels like it belongs in the future. It cost roughly 1.4 billion dollars to build. Here is the thing that makes Chase Center genuinely unusual: the Warriors paid for almost all of it themselves.

Most professional sports arenas are built using a combination of team money and public tax dollars, which is a nice way of saying the city chips in and taxpayers foot part of the bill. The Warriors decided to build Chase Center almost entirely with private funding. No public money. No asking the city of San Francisco to write a check. They bought the land, hired the architects, managed the construction, and opened the doors without leaning on the public to finance it. In the world of professional sports arena deals, that is extremely rare.

The arena sits on the Mission Bay waterfront and holds about 18,000 fans for basketball games. It also hosts concerts, events, and everything else a modern arena runs through its doors. The Warriors had previously played in Oakland at the Oracle Arena, which had been their home through the dynasty years and held some of the loudest crowds in the NBA. Leaving Oakland was not without controversy. But Chase Center became one of the most impressive venues in professional sports essentially from the day it opened. Sometimes spending 1.4 billion dollars on something works out exactly as planned.

19. The Death Lineup: Five Guys Who Broke Basketball (2015-2019)

In the 2015 NBA Finals, the Warriors were struggling against the Cleveland Cavaliers. Golden State coach Steve Kerr made a decision that looked strange on paper and turned out to be one of the most important tactical moves in modern basketball history. He moved Draymond Green to center and put five perimeter players on the floor at the same time. No traditional big man. No one taller than six feet eight. Just five smart, fast, switchable defenders who could all shoot and all pass.

They called it the Death Lineup. Cleveland had no answer for it. The Warriors could switch every screen without giving up an easy basket. They could shoot from anywhere. They could push the pace and punish slower lineups. The Death Lineup helped Golden State win the 2015 championship and became the blueprint for how modern NBA offenses think about spacing.

Before the Warriors started winning with small-ball lineups, the conventional wisdom was that you needed a big center to compete for a championship. A mountain in the middle. Someone to protect the rim and dominate the paint. The Warriors proved that if everyone on the floor is skilled enough and smart enough, you do not need the mountain. You just need five guys who can do everything. The entire league spent the next several years trying to figure out how to build their own version of the Death Lineup. Most of them are still working on it.

20. Steph Curry's Warmup: Why Arenas Fill Up Just to Watch Practice

Stephen Curry arrives at the arena before games and starts shooting. That sounds like a completely normal sentence. What is not normal is that opposing fans, the people who paid good money to watch their team beat the Warriors, show up early specifically to watch Curry warm up. Not to boo him. Not to distract him. To watch. Because Stephen Curry's pre-game shooting routine is genuinely worth the price of admission by itself.

The routine involves shooting from half court, from the logo, from places on the floor that are not technically shooting spots. It involves behind-the-back catches and releases, trick shots, and sequences where he makes fifteen three-pointers in a row from different spots without stopping to think. The whole thing looks less like an NBA player getting loose and more like someone showing off powers they probably should not have. People pull out their phones. Videos end up on social media. Crowds that are supposed to be hostile go quiet for a minute just to watch.

Curry has said the extended warmup is not just about shooting. It is about rhythm. About getting his body and mind locked into a groove before the game starts. It is also, if we are being honest, a little bit of a psychological operation. The other team's players watch too. They know what Curry can do. Watching him make half-court shots before tip-off is not exactly a confidence booster. The warmup that looks like a show is also a warning. And by the time the ball is actually tipped, everybody in the building has already seen what is possible.

Chapter 5: Now and Next

21. The Klay Thompson Era Ends: A Bittersweet Goodbye (2024)

Every great partnership eventually ends. In the summer of 2024, after thirteen seasons, four championships, five All-Star appearances, and one third quarter in Sacramento that will never be forgotten, Klay Thompson signed with the Dallas Mavericks. He was no longer a Golden State Warrior. The basketball world paused for a second and felt something.

Klay was not just a great player. He was the other half of one of the most beloved duos in NBA history. Curry and Thompson. The Splash Brothers. Two names that belonged together the way peanut butter belongs with jelly, except instead of sandwiches they made three-pointers and won championships. When Klay was healthy and locked in, opposing coaches lost sleep designing defenses specifically to keep him from touching the ball in certain spots on the floor. He was that kind of problem.

The split was not ugly. It was just the natural end of something that had run its course. Thompson had battled back from two devastating injuries, won that fourth ring in 2022, and given Golden State everything he had. Leaving was his choice, and Dallas offered him a new chapter. Warriors fans gave him a standing ovation when he returned to Chase Center in a Mavericks uniform. That is the right way to say goodbye to someone who helped build something special. Thirteen years. Four rings. One quarter that nobody will ever top. Not a bad run.

22. The Next Generation: Easier Said Than Done

Building a dynasty is hard. Rebuilding one while a legend is still on your roster might be even harder. The Golden State Warriors spent several years trying to figure out who the next piece of their future would be, and Jonathan Kuminga looked like the answer. Drafted seventh overall in 2021, the 23-year-old forward from the Democratic Republic of Congo had the athleticism, the size, and the highlight-reel ability that makes scouts write things like "franchise cornerstone" in their notebooks.

It never quite clicked. Kuminga had big games, including back-to-back 34-point performances in December 2024 that made Warriors fans very excited. But the fit with

Steve Kerr's system stayed complicated, the playing time went up and down, and by the trade deadline this season Golden State moved him to the Atlanta Hawks. Within weeks of joining Atlanta he was averaging 21 points and shooting nearly 68 percent from the field. Sometimes a player just needs a fresh start and a different stage.

The Warriors replaced him with Kristaps Porzingis, a seven-foot Latvian who can shoot threes and protect the rim, which is exactly the kind of player that fits next to Curry and Green. Moses Moody, 23, is still in the mix as a developing wing. The next generation of Warriors is still being assembled. That is not a crisis. That is just what the middle of a transition looks like. Every dynasty goes through one. The question is always the same: who are the next guys? Golden State is still working on the answer.

23. The Jimmy Butler Chapter: One More Swing (2025-present)

In February 2025, the Golden State Warriors made a move that turned heads across the league. They traded for Jimmy Butler, one of the most intense and competitive players in the NBA, a six-time All-Star with a reputation for showing up largest when the stakes are highest. The Warriors decided that pairing Butler with Curry and Green was worth the gamble. The basketball world leaned forward.

Butler is the kind of player who does not need the ball in his hands every possession to control a game. He defends. He attacks the basket. He draws fouls at a rate that makes opposing coaches want to take a long walk. He has made five All-Star teams and led the Miami Heat to the NBA Finals twice. He is not a finesse player. He is a problem. Putting him next to Curry, who stretches defenses to their absolute limit, creates a matchup nightmare that teams have to solve with almost no good options.

This is not the dominant dynasty team of 2017. It is a different kind of team. Older in some spots, hungrier in others, held together by the greatest shooter who ever lived and the most competitive defender of his generation. Golden State has already proved it can rebuild around Curry once. The question is whether this version of the Warriors has enough left to capture one more championship before the window closes for good. It would not be the first time this franchise surprised everyone. It probably will not be the last.

24. Seven Banners and Counting: Where Does This Team Rank All-Time?

Seven championships. That is where the Golden State Warriors sit in the all-time record books, third behind the Boston Celtics and Los Angeles Lakers. They won the very first championship this league ever handed out in 1947. They have won in Philadelphia, in San Francisco, and in Oakland. They have won with Wilt Chamberlain setting records nobody could touch and with Stephen Curry rewriting the record books in a completely different direction sixty years later. That is a remarkable arc for one franchise.

The dynasty years from 2015 to 2022 changed how people think about Golden State. Before that run, the Warriors were a franchise with a complicated history: some early success, a long middle stretch of struggling, a few exciting but ringless teams, and a lot of years where the playoffs felt far away. Four championships in eight years turned them into something different. It turned them into a conversation about the greatest teams ever.

Here is the honest truth about where the Warriors rank. The Celtics have eighteen championships. The Lakers have seventeen. Nobody is catching them anytime soon, including Golden State. But within the conversation about the most influential franchises in basketball history, the Warriors belong. They won the first title. They changed the modern game. They produced one of the most dominant dynasties of the last thirty years. Three different eras, three different versions of greatness, all wearing the same blue and gold. Not many franchises can say that.

25. The Bay Always Bounces Back

Here is something the history of the Golden State
Warriors teaches you if you pay close enough attention.
This franchise has never stayed down for long. They lost
Wilt Chamberlain and dropped to 17 wins. Then Rick
Barry showed up and they swept Washington for a
championship. They went through a decade of losing in
the 1980s. Then Run TMC showed up and made the Bay
fall in love with basketball again. They missed the
playoffs for thirteen straight years. Then We Believe
happened. Then the whole dynasty happened.

The Warriors have been to nine NBA Finals. They have
won seven championships across eight decades. They
have played in three different cities under multiple
different names and found a way to matter in every era.
That is not luck. That is something built into the culture
of the organization.

Right now the Warriors are in transition. The Splash
Brothers era is officially over with Klay gone. Curry is 37
and the clock on his career is ticking, even if his shot still
sounds like a clock nobody wants to stop. The young
pieces around him are still figuring out who they are
going to become. The next chapter is not fully written
yet. But if you have been paying attention to eighty

years of Warriors history, you already know how this kind of story tends to go. The Bay always bounces back. And somewhere in the future, there is another banner waiting to be hung at Chase Center. Golden State just has to go get it.

Bonus Trivia Quiz!

You think you are a true Warriors fan? Try this bonus quiz!

1. The Philadelphia Warriors won the very first championship in league history. What year was that?

A) 1944

B) 1947

C) 1951

D) 1955

2. Wilt Chamberlain's famous 100-point game was played in which unusual location?

A) Madison Square Garden in New York

B) The Cow Palace in San Francisco

C) A hockey rink in Hershey, Pennsylvania

D) The Philadelphia Spectrum

3. What was the width of the NBA lane before George Mikan forced the league to change it?

A) 6 feet

B) 8 feet

C) 10 feet

D) 12 feet

4. The Warriors swept which team in the 1975 NBA Finals in one of the biggest upsets in league history?

A) Boston Celtics

B) Los Angeles Lakers

C) New York Knicks

D) Washington Bullets

5. What was the nickname of the Warriors trio of Tim Hardaway, Mitch Richmond, and Chris Mullin?

A) The Bay Brothers

B) Run TMC

C) The Golden Three

D) Splash and Friends

6. Stephen Curry became the first unanimous MVP in NBA history in which season?

A) 2013-14

B) 2014-15

C) 2015-16

D) 2016-17

7. How many three-pointers did Curry make in the record-breaking 2015-16 season?

A) 286

B) 325

C) 369

D) 402

8. How many points did Klay Thompson score in his record-breaking third quarter against the Sacramento Kings in 2015?

A) 29

B) 33

C) 37

D) 41

9. What was the Warriors' win-loss record during the historic 2015-16 regular season?

A) 69-13

B) 70-12

C) 72-10

D) 73-9

10. What did Warriors coach Steve Kerr name the revolutionary small-ball lineup he used during the 2015 Finals?

A) The Small Five
B) The Death Lineup
C) The Speed Squad
D) The Splash Formation

11. The "We Believe" Warriors pulled off a stunning first-round upset in 2007 against which heavily favored opponent?

A) San Antonio Spurs
B) Los Angeles Lakers
C) Dallas Mavericks
D) Phoenix Suns

12. Approximately how much did the Warriors spend building Chase Center, almost entirely with private funding?

A) 500 million dollars
B) 800 million dollars
C) 1.4 billion dollars
D) 2.1 billion dollars

13. How old was Stephen Curry during the 2025-26 NBA season?

A) 34

B) 35

C) 36

D) 37

14. Which former Warriors player won the 1975 NBA Finals MVP award after averaging 29.5 points per game in the series?

A) Jamaal Wilkes

B) Al Attles

C) Nate Thurmond

D) Rick Barry

15. Jonathan Kuminga was born in which country?

A) Nigeria

B) Cameroon

C) Democratic Republic of Congo

D) Senegal

Super Fan Secret Challenge

Only a true Warriors fan will know this.

(No Answer Provided)

Wilt Chamberlain held the NBA record for most points in a single game with 100 for over 60 years. As of March 2026, who holds the second-highest single-game scoring record in NBA history, and how many points did they score?

Answer Key

1. B) 1947

2. C) A hockey rink in Hershey, Pennsylvania

3. A) 6 feet

4. D) Washington Bullets

5. B) Run TMC

6. C) 2015-16

7. D) 402

8. C) 37

9. D) 73-9

10. B) The Death Lineup

11. C) Dallas Mavericks

12. C) 1.4 billion dollars

13. D) 37

14. D) Rick Barry

15. C) Democratic Republic of Congo

NBA PLAYOFF BRACKET

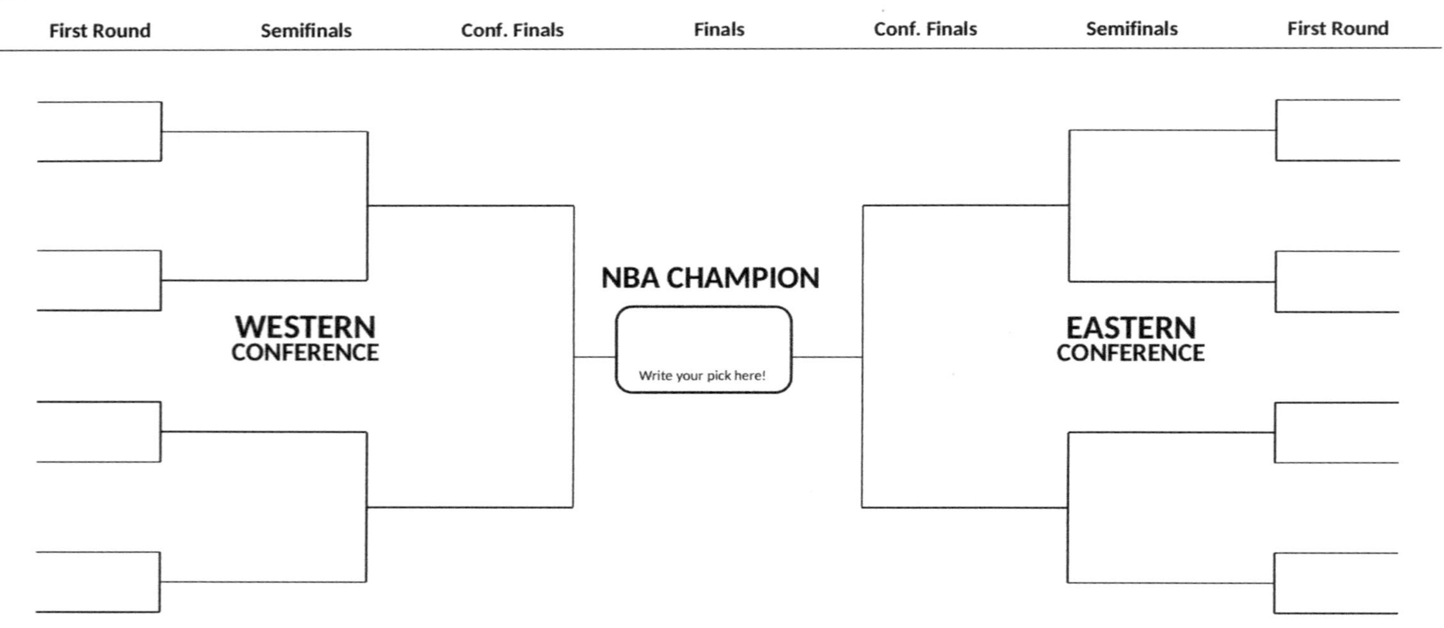

* Fill in your picks and try not to argue with your friends about it!

Part of the Fun Fan Facts: The Unofficial Sports Guide Series

Be the Boss of the Playoffs

You've broken down the matchups. You know which superstar takes over in the fourth quarter. You've seen the bench units that quietly decide series. You've watched the adjustments coaches make when their backs are against the wall.

Now it's time to stop watching and start deciding.

On this page, you are not just a fan. You are the Head Coach drawing up the last play with three seconds left on the clock. You are the GM who built this roster. You are the analyst who saw it all coming.

This is not just filling out a bracket.

This is building your championship run.

Sixteen teams enter the NBA Playoffs. The path is brutal. Best of seven. No shortcuts. No hiding. Every round gets louder, harder, and more personal.

This bracket is your Playoff Control Room.

The Game Plan

1. Survive Round One: Start with the opening round. Which matchup is going seven games? Who has the closer? Who folds under pressure? Make the calls.

2. Feel the Momentum: As you move into the Conference Semifinals and Conference Finals, things change. Role players become heroes. Stars feel the weight. Trust your reads.

3. Own the Finals: Trace your picks all the way to the NBA Finals. When the confetti falls and the trophy is raised, you'll find out who earned it.

House Rules: Circle your boldest upset. That is your official "I knew it" moment.

Choose Your Weapon: Pencil if you want flexibility. Pen if you trust your instincts. Sharpie if you believe in chaos.

Because once the playoffs tip off, there is no rewinding Game 7.

Make your picks. Trust your basketball brain. And let the playoff drama begin.

Fun Facts Wrap-Up

You made it through! You're officially a true superfan! Now it's time to put your knowledge to the test. Share these facts with friends and see who really knows their team best.

Love the series?

Your reviews help other fans discover Fun Fan Facts. If you enjoyed this book, we'd really appreciate you sharing your thoughts and leaving a review.

Want more Fun Fan Facts?

Scan the QR code below to visit our site and explore bonus trivia, challenges, and special extras - including new teams, future series, and collectible fun as they're released.

Collect All the Fun Fan Facts Series!

Check off every book you read. See the full set on Amazon. Search "Fun Fan Facts Jake Liam."

World Cup 2026 Edition

☐ Algeria	☐ Scotland	☐ Morocco
☐ France	☐ Brazil	☐ Switzerland
☐ Paraguay	☐ Ivory Coast	☐ Curaçao
☐ Argentina	☐ Senegal	☐ Netherlands
☐ Germany	☐ Canada	☐ Tunisia
☐ Portugal	☐ Japan	☐ Ecuador
☐ Australia	☐ South Africa	☐ New Zealand
☐ Ghana	☐ Cape Verde	☐ United States
☐ Qatar	☐ Jordan	☐ Egypt
☐ Austria	☐ South Korea	☐ Norway
☐ Haiti	☐ Colombia	☐ Uruguay
☐ Saudi Arabia	☐ Mexico	☐ England
☐ Belgium	☐ Spain	☐ Panama
☐ Iran	☐ Croatia	☐ Uzbekistan

World Cup 2026 Group Edition

☐ Group A	☐ Group F	☐ Group K
☐ Group E	☐ Group J	☐ Group D
☐ Group I	☐ Group C	☐ Group H
☐ Group B	☐ Group G	☐ Group L

English Football Edition

- ☐ Arsenal F.C.
- ☐ Aston Villa F.C.
- ☐ Chelsea F.C.
- ☐ Everton F.C.
- ☐ Fulham F.C.
- ☐ Liverpool F.C.
- ☐ Manchester City
- ☐ Manchester United
- ☐ Newcastle United F.C.
- ☐ Tottenham Hotspur
- ☐ West Ham United
- ☐ Wrexham A.F.C.

NBA Edition

- ☐ Atlanta Hawks
- ☐ Boston Celtics
- ☐ Brooklyn Nets
- ☐ Charlotte Hornets
- ☐ Chicago Bulls
- ☐ Cleveland Cavaliers
- ☐ Dallas Mavericks
- ☐ Denver Nuggets
- ☐ Detroit Pistons
- ☐ Golden State Warriors
- ☐ Houston Rockets
- ☐ Indiana Pacers
- ☐ LA Clippers
- ☐ Los Angeles Lakers
- ☐ Memphis Grizzlies
- ☐ Miami Heat
- ☐ Milwaukee Bucks
- ☐ Minnesota Timberwolves
- ☐ New Orleans Pelicans
- ☐ New York Knicks
- ☐ Oklahoma City Thunder
- ☐ Orlando Magic
- ☐ Philadelphia 76ers
- ☐ Phoenix Suns
- ☐ Portland Trail Blazers
- ☐ Sacramento Kings
- ☐ San Antonio Spurs
- ☐ Toronto Raptors
- ☐ Utah Jazz
- ☐ Washington Wizards

About the Author

Jake is a 13-year-old sports fan who loves football, American football, and basketball. He plays soccer as a goalie and dreams of one day playing for West Ham United and helping teach kids to love the game. His passion for sports runs in the family - his dad was a professional baseball player, and his stepdad sparked his love for West Ham. Through the Fun Fan Facts series, he shares the fun and excitement of sports with fans everywhere.